Piano · Vocal · Guitar

THE BEST CLASSIC ROCK SONGS EVER

ISBN 0-634-03648-3

HAL•LEONARD®
CORPORATION

7777 W. BLUEMOUND RD. P.O. BOX 13819 MILWAUKEE, WI 53213

Visit Hal Leonard Online at
www.halleonard.com

AMERICAN WOMAN

Written by BURTON CUMMINGS,
RANDY BACHMAN, GARY PETERSON and JIM KALE

wo - man, _____ lis - ten what I say. _____

Don't come hang - ing 'round _ my door; _

don't wan - na see your face _ no more. _ I don't need your war _

_ ma - chines. _ I don't need your ghet - to scenes. _

BAD CASE OF LOVING YOU

Words and Music by
JOHN MOON MARTIN

Whoa.

The hot sum-mer night ___

fell like a net.
don't make no pret-ty heart; ___
by twen-ty-one to zip, ___

I've got-ta
I learned
Smile of

BADGE

Words and Music by ERIC CLAPTON
and GEORGE HARRISON

BANG A GONG
(Get It On)

Words and Music by
MARC BOLAN

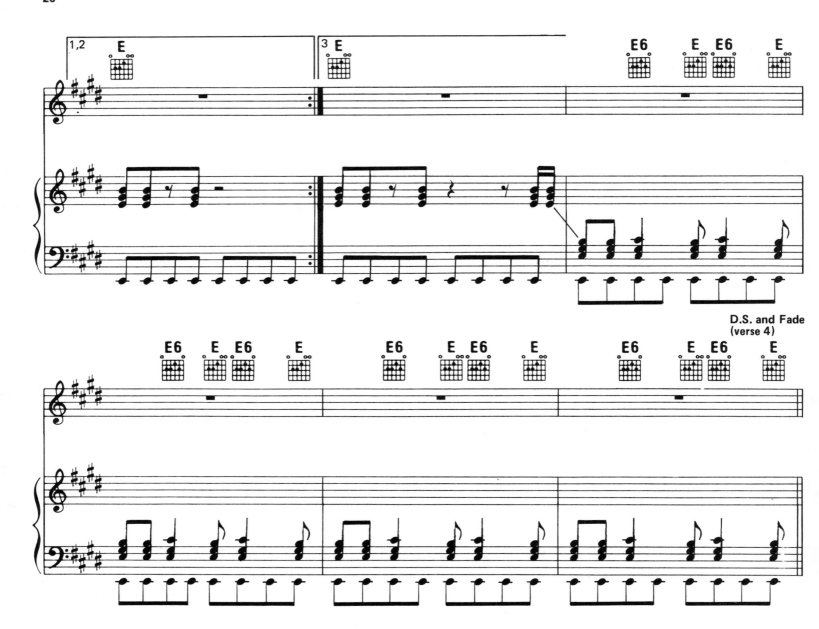

D.S. and Fade
(verse 4)

2. You're built like a car
You've got a hub cap diamond star halo
You're built like a car oh yeah
You're an untamed youth that's the truth
With your cloak full of eagles
You're dirty sweet and you're my girl.

3. You're windy and wild
You've got the blues in your shoes and your stockings
You're windy and wild oh yeah
You're built like a car
You've got a hub cap diamond star halo
You're dirty sweet and you're my girl.

4. You're dirty and sweet
Clad in black, don't look back and I love you.
You're dirty and sweet oh yeah
You dance when you walk
So let's dance, take a chance, understand me
You're dirty sweet and you're my girl.

To Chorus and Fade

BARRACUDA

Words and Music by ROGER FISHER,
NANCY WILSON, ANN WILSON and MICHAEL DEROSIER

Moderately fast

THE BITCH IS BACK

Words and Music by ELTON JOHN
and BERNIE TAUPIN

With a driving beat

BRAIN DAMAGE

Words and Music by
ROGER WATERS

BRASS IN POCKET

Words and Music by CHRISSIE HYNDE
and JAMES HONEYMAN-SCOTT

Moderate Rock

CAN'T YOU SEE

Words and Music by
TOY CALDWELL

Gon - na take a freight _ train down at the sta - tion, Lord. _
I'm gon - na find _ me a hole in the wall; _
I'm gon - na buy a tick - et as far as I can; _

I don't care where it goes. _
gon - na crawl in side and die, _
I ain't - a nev - er com - in' back. _

Gon - na climb a moun - tain, the high - est moun - tain, Lord, _
'cause my la - dy, now a mean old wom - an, Lord, _
I'm gon - na take me that south - bound, ride it all the way to Geor - gia, Lord, _

CAUGHT UP IN YOU

Words and Music by FRANK SULLIVAN, JIM PETERIK,
JEFF CARLISI and DON BARNES

DON'T DO ME LIKE THAT

Words and Music by
TOM PETTY

Moderately

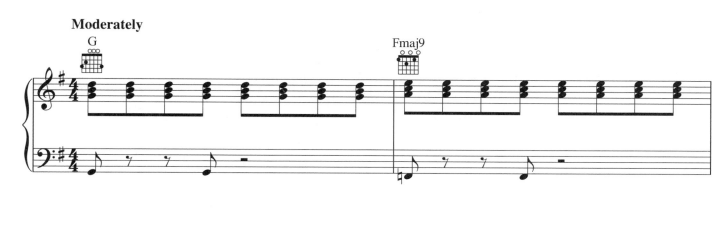

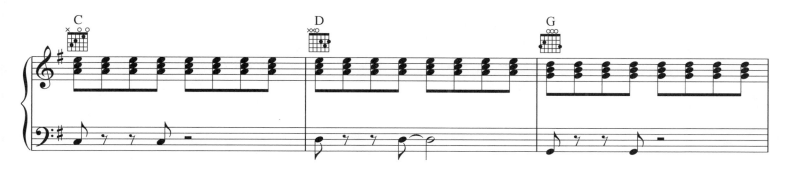

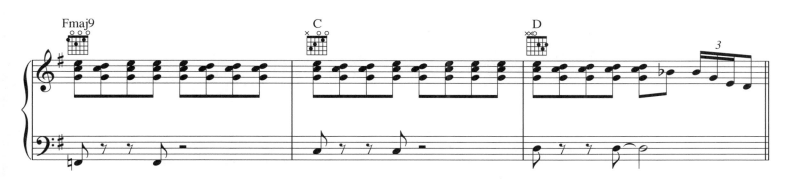

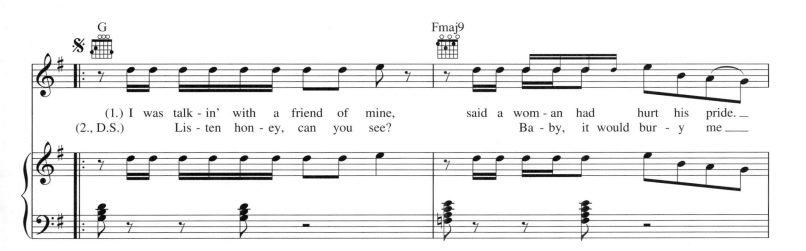

(1.) I was talk-in' with a friend of mine, said a wom-an had hurt his pride. __
(2., D.S.) Lis-ten hon-ey, can you see? Ba-by, it would bur-y me __

CHANGES

Words and Music by
DAVID BOWIE

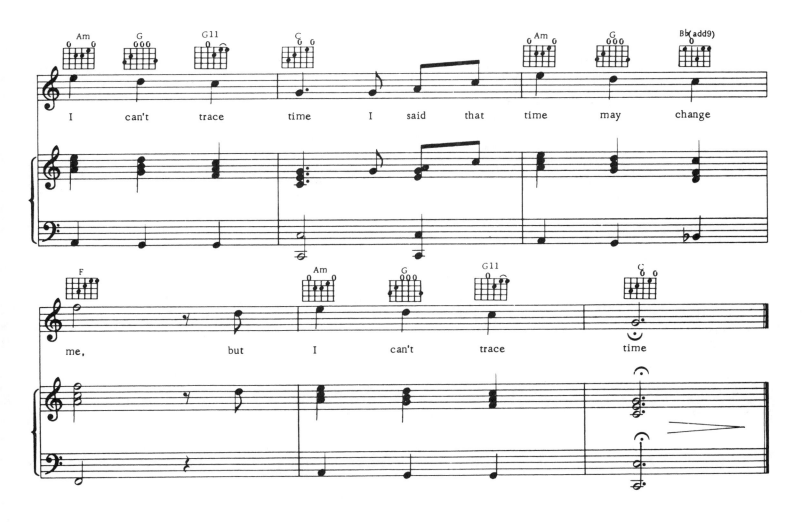

I can't trace time I said that time may change me, but I can't trace time

Verse 2.

I watch the ripples change their size, but never leave the stream
Of warm impermanence and so the days flow thru my eyes
But still the days seem the same.
And these children that you spit on as they try to change their worlds
Are immune to your consultations, they're quite aware of what they're going thru'

(Chorus 2.)

(Ch-ch-ch-ch-Changes) Turn and face the stranger -
(Ch-ch-changes) Don't tell them to grow up and out of it,
(Ch-ch-ch-ch-changes) Turn and face the stranger
(Ch- ch-changes) where's your shame, you've left us up to our necks in it
Time may change me, but you can't trace time.   (To Interlude)

COLD AS ICE

Words and Music by MICK JONES
and LOU GRAMM

COME SAIL AWAY

Words and Music by
DENNIS DE YOUNG

DAY TRIPPER

Words and Music by JOHN LENNON
and PAUL McCARTNEY

Moderate Rock

E7

Got a good rea - son
She's a big tea - ser,
Tried to please_ her,

for

DON'T FEAR THE REAPER

Words and Music by
DONALD ROESER

D.S. al Coda

CODA

Repeat and Fade

DREAMER

Words and Music by RICK DAVIES
and ROGER HODGSON

Moderately fast

Dream - er, you know you are a dream - er. Well, can you put your hands in your head, oh no! I said dream - er, you're noth-ing but a

you can do some-thing.) If I could do an-y-thing... (But can you do some - thing

out ____ of this world?) ____

Take a dream on a Sun - day.

cresc. little by little

EASY LOVER

Words and Music by PHIL COLLINS,
PHILIP BAILEY and NATHAN EAST

Eas - y lov - er. She'll get a hold on you, be - lieve — it,

EMOTIONAL RESCUE

Words and Music by MICK JAGGER
and KEITH RICHARDS

rich man's house. ___ Oo oo oo oo oo oo oo oo. ___

Oo oo oo oo oo oo oo oo. ___ Yeah,

ba - by, I'm cry - ing o - ver you.

Don't you know prom-is-es ___ were nev-er meant to keep?
You think you're one of a spe - cial breed.
I come to you so si - lent in the night,

Just like the night, they dis -
You think that you're his
so stealth - y, so

mine, _   mine, _   oo.

(Spoken:) Yes, you could be mine

tonight and every night.

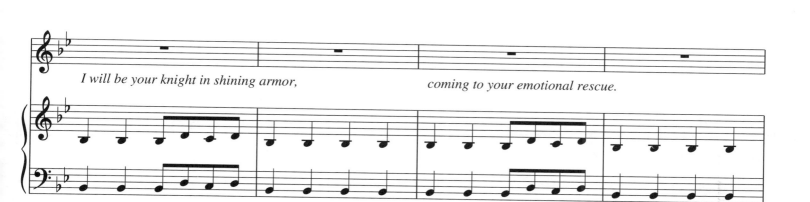

I will be your knight in shining armor,   *coming to your emotional rescue.*

Repeat and Fade

You will be mine, you will be mine, all mine.

EYE IN THE SKY

Words and Music by ALAN PARSONS
and ERIC WOOLFSON

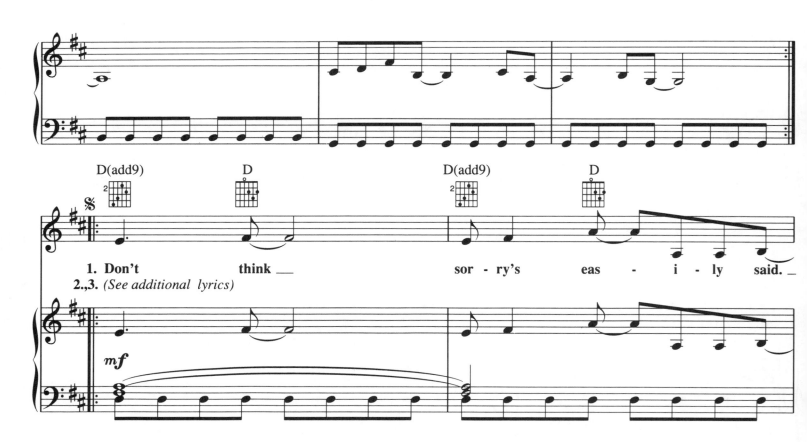

Additional Lyrics

2. Don't say words you're gonna regret.
   Don't let the fire rush to your head.
   I've heard the accusation before,
   And I ain't gonna take any more,
   Believe me.
   The sun in your eyes
   Made some of the lies worth believing.
   (To Chorus:)

3. Don't leave false illusions behind.
   Don't cry 'cause I ain't changing my mind.
   So find another fool like before,
   'Cause I ain't gonna live anymore believing
   Some of the lies, while all of the signs are deceiving.
   (To Chorus:)

HEARTACHE TONIGHT

Words and Music by JOHN DAVID SOUTHER, DON HENLEY, GLENN FREY and BOB SEGER

know. ___ There'll be a heart - ache to-night, ___ a heart-ache to-night, I know. ___

FREE RIDE

Words and Music by
DAN HARTMAN

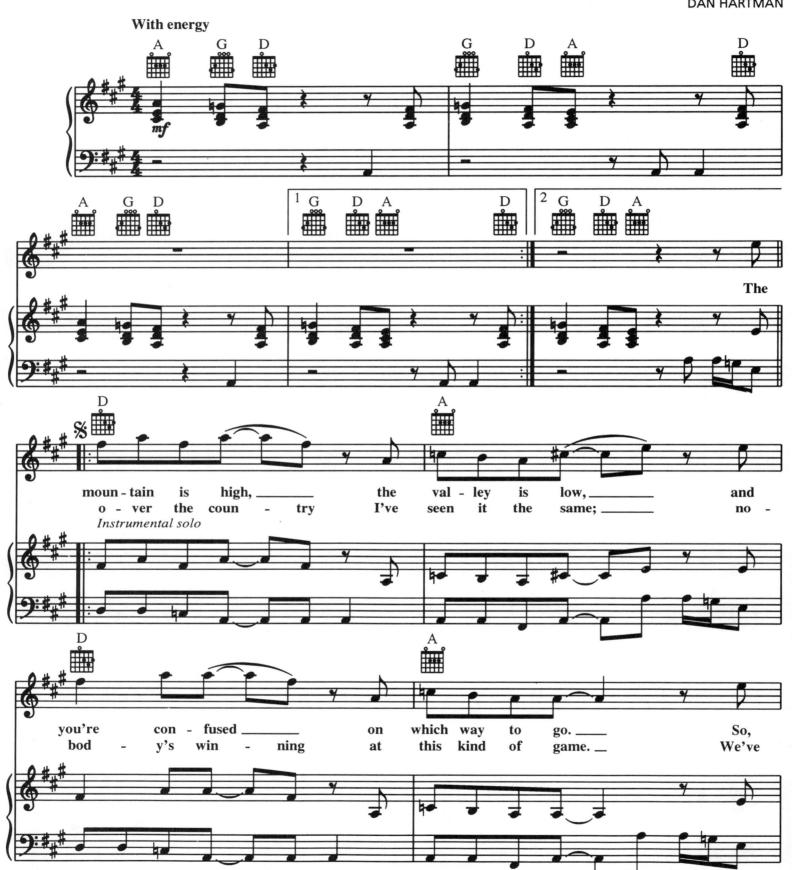

Come on ___ and take a free ride.

All Yeah, yeah, yeah, yeah.

CODA

HEAT OF THE MOMENT

Words and Music by GEOFFREY DOWNES
and JOHN WETTON

I nev-er meant to be so bad___ to you,

one thing I said that I would nev - er do.

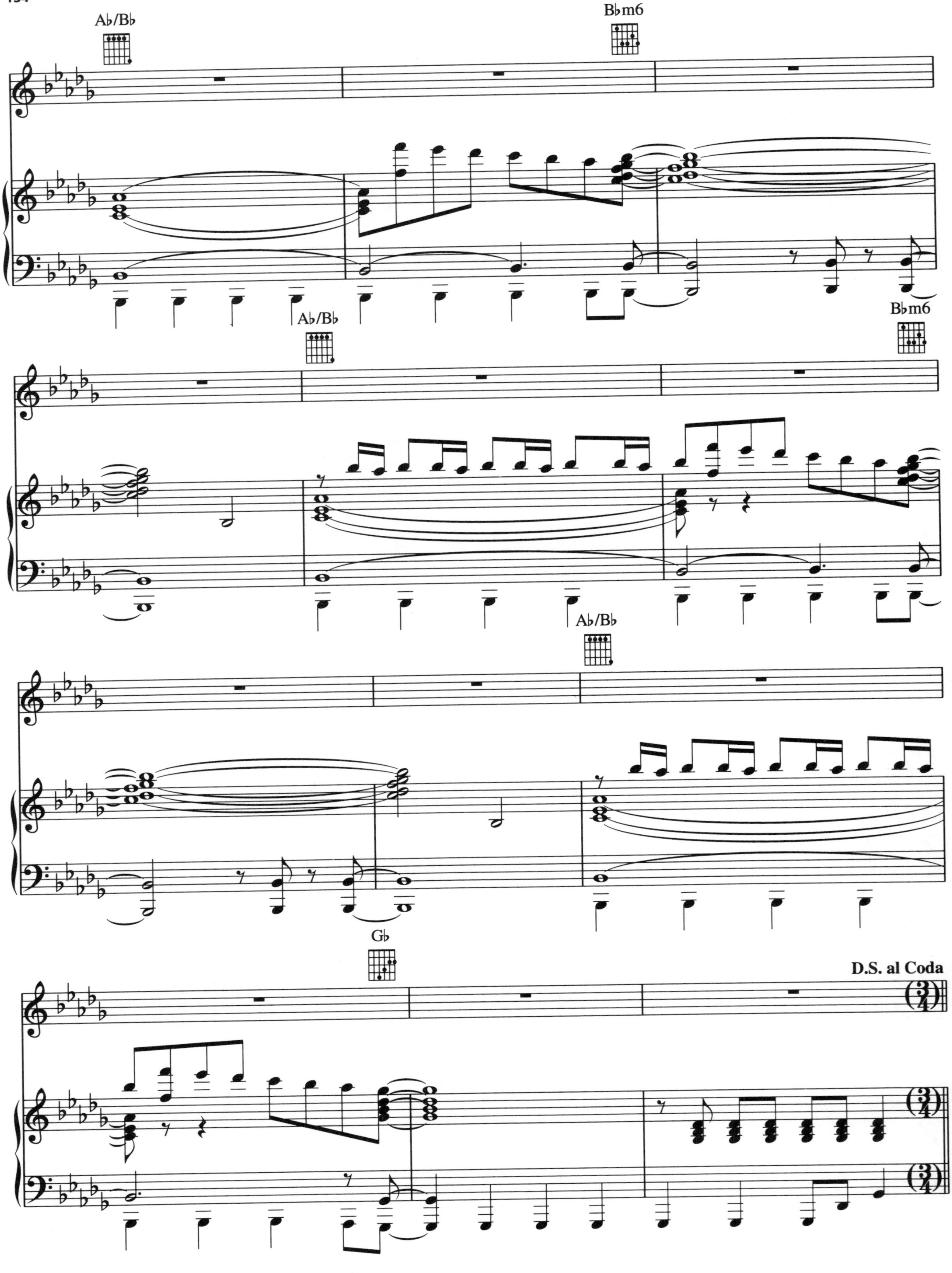
A♭/B♭
B♭m6
A♭/B♭
B♭m6
A♭/B♭
G♭
D.S. al Coda

HEY JOE

Words and Music by
BILLY ROBERTS

THE HOUSE IS ROCKIN'

Written by STEVIE RAY VAUGHAN
and DOYLE BRAMHALL

Fast Rock 'n' Roll

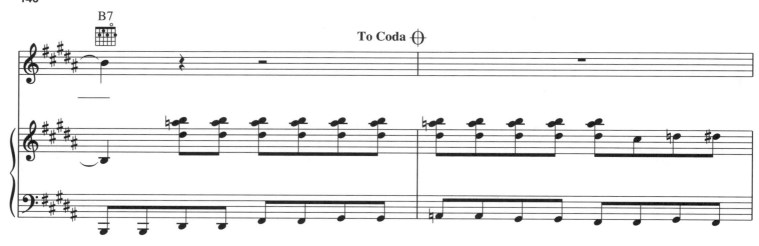

I CAN SEE FOR MILES

Words and Music by
PETER TOWNSHEND

Bright Rock

I know you've de-ceived me. Now here's a sur-prise.

I know that you have 'cos there's ma-gic in___ my

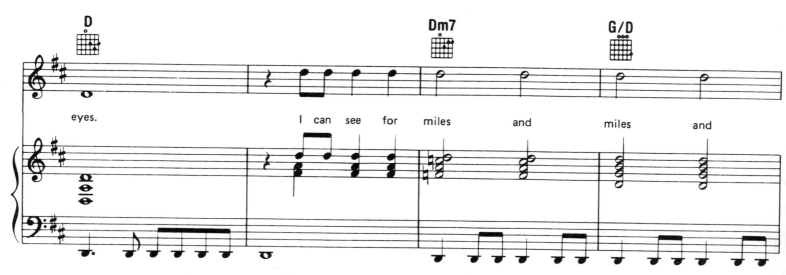

eyes. I can see for miles and miles and

I JUST WANT TO MAKE LOVE TO YOU

Written by WILLIE DIXON

I WANT TO KNOW WHAT LOVE IS

Words and Music by
MICK JONES

I WANT YOU TO WANT ME

Words and Music by
RICK NIELSEN

I want you to want me. I

need you to need me. I'd

159

IF YOU LEAVE ME NOW

Words and Music by
PETER CETERA

D.S. al Coda
(with repeats)

JACK AND DIANE

Words and Music by
JOHN MELLENCAMP

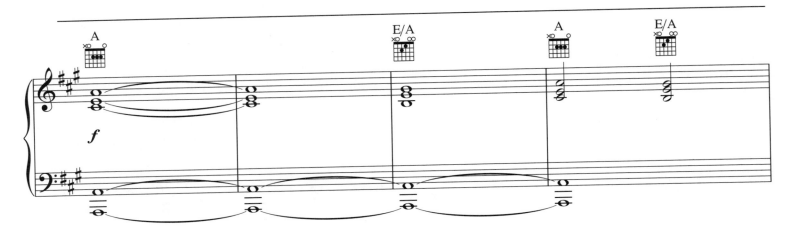

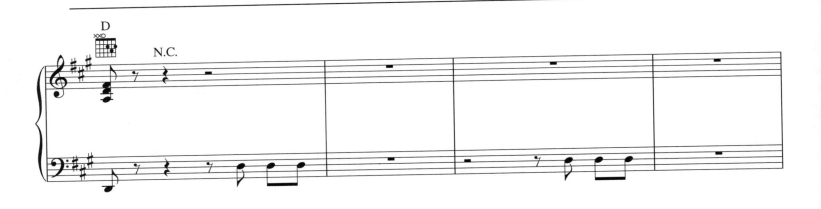

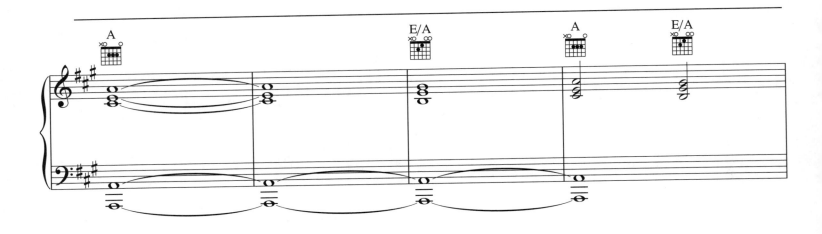

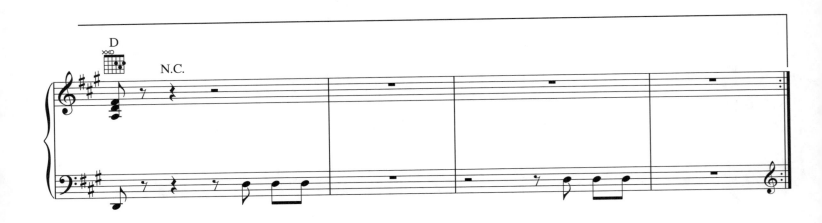

dit - ty   a - bout   Jack   and   Di -   ane, _____

two   A - mer - i - can   kids   do - in'   the   best   that   they __   can.

f

N.C.

Repeat and Fade

INVISIBLE TOUCH

Words and Music by TONY BANKS,
PHIL COLLINS and MIKE RUTHERFORD

IT'S STILL ROCK AND ROLL TO ME

Words and Music by
BILLY JOEL

Moderately Fast

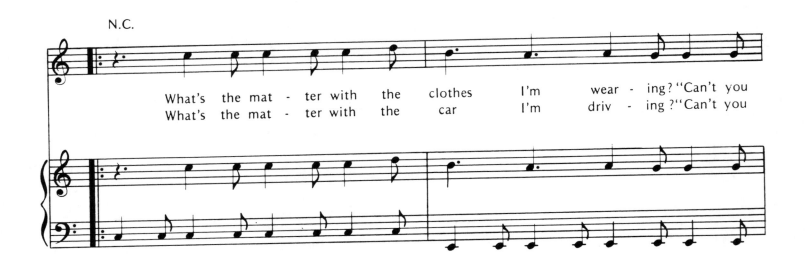

What's the mat - ter with the clothes I'm wear - ing? "Can't you
What's the mat - ter with the car I'm driv - ing? "Can't you

tell that your tie's too wide?"
tell that it's out of style?"

Ooh, _____

D. S. 𝄉 *al Coda* ⊕

Coda C

N.C.
Ev - 'ry - bod - y's talk - in' 'bout the new sound. Fun - ny, but it's

still rock and roll to me. _____

C9

THE LOCO-MOTION

Words and Music by GERRY GOFFIN
and CAROLE KING

LOVE STINKS

Words and Music by SETH JUSTMAN
and PETER WOLF

You love her, but she loves him, and he loves some-bod-y else. You just can't win. And You'll

Two by two and side by side, love's gon-na find you, yes it is. You just can't hide. And You'll

MESSAGE IN A BOTTLE

Written and Composed by
STING

ONCE BITTEN TWICE SHY

Words and Music by
IAN HUNTER

Moderate Rock Beat

Well the times are get-tin' hard for you ___ lit-tle girl. I'm a
mid-dle of the night on the o-pen road. ___ The
wom-an you're a mess, gon-na die in your sleep. There's
Instrumental

PINK HOUSES

Words and Music by
JOHN MELLENCAMP

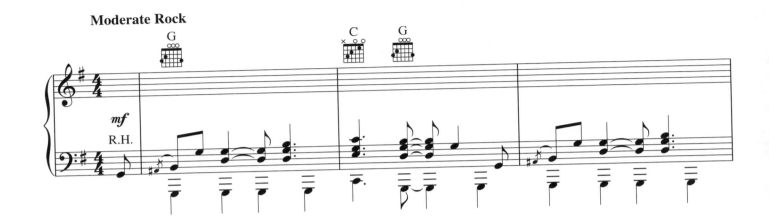

There's a   black man   with a black cat
young man   in   a   T - shirt
peo - ple   and more peo - ple.

liv - in' in a black neigh - bor - hood. _____   He's got an
lis - t'nin' to a rock - in' roll - in' sta - tion. _____   He's got
What   do   they   know? _____

in - ter - state ___ run - nin' through ___ his front yard. ___ You know, he
greas - y hair ___ and a greas - y smile ___ that says, "Lord,
Go to work ___ in some high - rise and va - ca - tion down at

F   C   G

thinks he's got it so good. _____
this must be my des - ti - na - tion."
the Gulf of Mex - i - co. _____

And there's a
'Cause they
And there's

wom - an in the kitch - en clean - in' up the eve - nin' slop. ___
told me when I was young - er, "Boy, you gon - na be Pres - i -
win - ners and there's los - ers, but they ain't no big deal. ___

RADAR LOVE

Words and Music by GEORGE KOOYMANS
and BARRY HAY

drives my heel. ____
com-in' on strong. _
got-ta take care. ____

It's my ba -
The road _
Last _

_ by call - in', said, "I need _ you here." _
__ has got _ me hyp-no - tized. _
__ car to pass, here _ I go. ____

And it's half past four and I'm shift - in' gear. _____
And I'll be spit - ting in - to a new sun - rise. _____
And the line of cars drove down real slow. _____

The ra - dar

Play 4 times

love. _

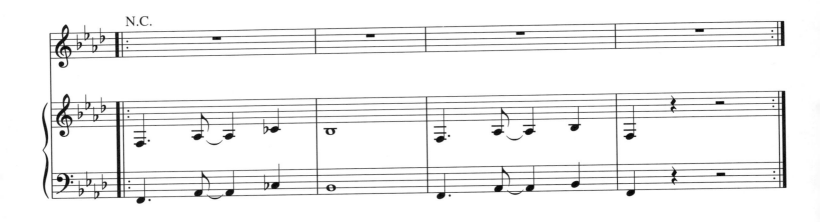

that's   called _____   ra - dar   love. _

REFUGEE

Words and Music by TOM PETTY
and MIKE CAMPBELL

RENEGADE

Words and Music by
TOMMY SHAW

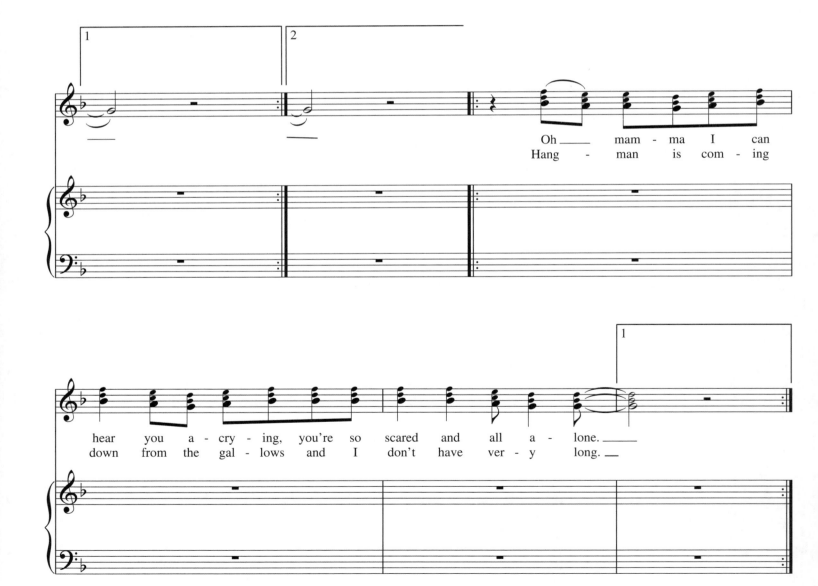

228

this will be the end to-day of the want-ed man, want-ed man.

Guitar solo ad lib.

Repeat and Fade

Optional Ending

RHIANNON

Words and Music by
STEVIE NICKS

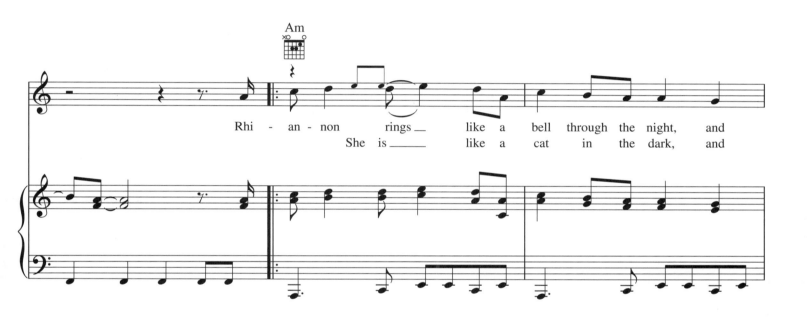

Rhi - an - non rings ___ like a bell through the night, and
She is ___ like a cat in the dark, and

would - n't you love to love ___ her? ___ Takes to the sky like a
then she is the dark - ness. ___ She rules her life like a

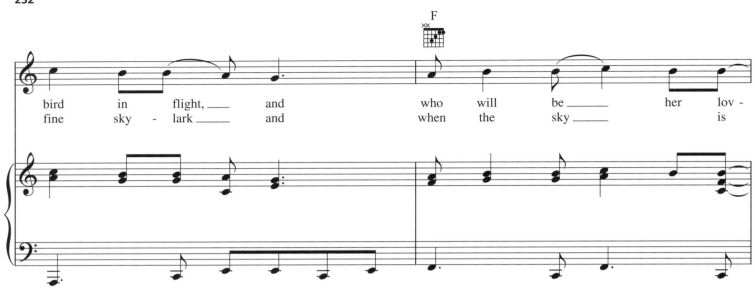

bird in flight, ____ and
fine sky - lark ____ and

who will be _____ her lov -
when the sky _____ is

- er?
star - less.

All your life ____ you've nev - er seen ____ a wom - an ____

____ tak - en by the wind. ____

Would you stay ____ if she prom -

RIDIN' THE STORM OUT

Words and Music by
GARY RICHRATH

RUN TO YOU

Words and Music by BRYAN ADAMS
and JIM VALLANCE

Oh, __ when the feel - in's right __ I'm gon - na run all night, __ I'm gon - na

run to you. _____

SCHOOL'S OUT

Words and Music by ALICE COOPER, NEAL SMITH, MICHAEL BRUCE,
GLEN BUXTON and DENNIS DUNAWAY

books. _____ No more teach - er's

dirt - y looks. _____ Out for

sum - mer, out till fall. _____

We might not come back at

SHAKEDOWN

from the Paramount Motion Picture BEVERLY HILLS COP II

Words and Music by KEITH FORSEY,
HAROLD FALTERMEYER and BOB SEGER

No mat-ter what you think you've pulled
how the race is won
town where ev-'ry-one

___ you'll find ___ it's not e-nough. ___
___ it al-ways ends the same. ___
___ is reach-in, for the top. ___

No mat-ter
An-oth-er
This is a

Let down your guard, hon - ey, just ___ a - bout the time you think that it's al - right. ___

Break - down, take - down; you're bust - ed. ___

SHOW ME THE WAY

Words and Music by
PETER FRAMPTON

Moderately

I won-der how__ you're feel-ing.__ There's
I can see__ no rea-son.__ You're

SOMEBODY TO LOVE

Words and Music by
DARBY SLICK

When the truth is found _ to be _

_ lies, and all _ the joy _

with - in you _ dies, don't you _

want some - bod - y to love? ___ Don't _ you _ need _ some - bod - y to love? _

Would - n't you ___ love some - bod - y to love? ___

You _ bet - ter find ___ some - bod - y to love. ___

SIGN OF THE GYPSY QUEEN

Words and Music by
LORENCE HUD

Sign of the Gyp-sy Queen;___ pack your things and leave.___

Word of a wom-an who knows:___ "Take all your gold and you go."___

SMOKE ON THE WATER

Words and Music by RITCHIE BLACKMORE, IAN GILLAN,
ROGER GLOVER, JON LORD and IAN PAICE

Heavy Rock

We all came out to Mon-
They burned down the gam-
We end-ed up at the Grand

THE STORY IN YOUR EYES

Words and Music by
JUSTIN HAYWARD

I've been think-in' 'bout __ our for - tune __ and I've de -
fright - ened for __ your chil - dren __ that the
fright - ened for __ your chil - dren __ that the

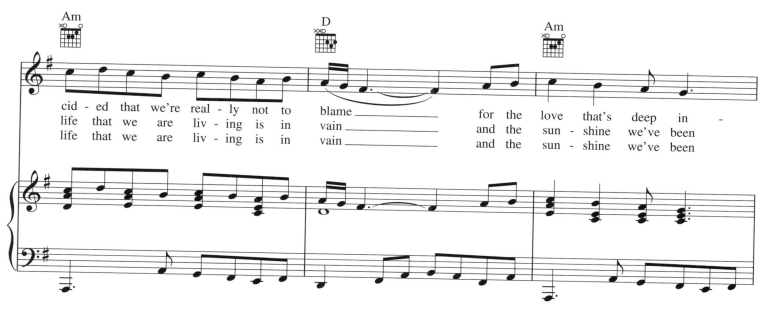

cid - ed that we're real - ly not to blame __ for the love that's deep in -
life that we are liv - ing is in vain __ and the sun - shine we've been
life that we are liv - ing is in vain __ and the sun - shine we've been

side us now __ is still the same. __ And the
wait - ing for __ will turn to rain. __ *Instrumental*
wait - ing for __ will turn to rain. __ When the

(So)
TIRED OF WAITING FOR YOU

Words and Music by
RAY DAVIES

Moderato

SUSIE-Q

Words and Music by DALE HAWKINS,
STAN LEWIS and ELEANOR BROADWATER

SWEET EMOTION

Words and Music by STEVEN TYLER
and TOM HAMILTON

You're call - in' my name but I
Well, I got good news, she's a
You're tell - in' her things but your
I'm talk - in' 'bout some-thin' you can

got - ta make clear. _____ 'cause my
real good li - ar, you
girl - friend lied; _____ 'cause a
sure un - der - stand, _____

can't say, ba - by, where I'll be in a year. _____
back - stage boo - gie set your pants on fire. _____
can't catch me 'cause the rab - bit done died. _____
month on the road and I'll be eat - in' from your hand. _____

TUMBLING DICE

Words and Music by MICK JAGGER
and KEITH RICHARDS

295

WE'RE READY

Words and Music by
TOM SCHOLZ

TURN ME LOOSE

Words and Music by PAUL DEAN
and DUKE RENO

I was born to run, ___ I was born to dream; ___ the
came a - round, ___ tried to tie me down. ___ I
here to please, I'm e - ven on my knees ___ mak - in'

WALK ON THE WILD SIDE

Words and Music by
LOU REED

WHEEL IN THE SKY

Words and Music by ROBERT FLEISCHMAN, NEAL SCHON
and DIANE VALORY

Win-ter is here ___ a-gain ___ oh Lord
I been try-in' to make it home ___

WITH A LITTLE HELP
FROM MY FRIENDS

Words and Music by JOHN LENNON
and PAUL McCARTNEY

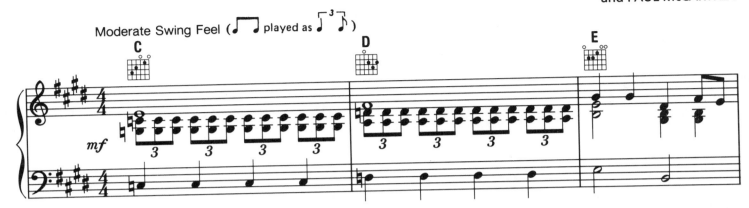

What would you do ___ if I sang ___ out of tune? ___ Would you stand ___
What do I do ___ when my love ___ is a-way? ___ (Does it wor-
(Would you be-lieve ___ in a love ___ at first sight?) ___ Yes I'm cer-

___ up and walk ___ out on me? ___
-ry you to be a - lone?) ___
-tain that it hap-pens all the time.

Lend me your ears ___ and I'll sing ___
How do I feel ___ by the end ___
(What do you see ___ when you turn

you a song___ and I'll try___ not to sing___ out of key.
of the day?___ (Are you sad___ be-cause you're on out of your own?)___
out the light?)___ I can't tell___ you, but I know___ it's mine.

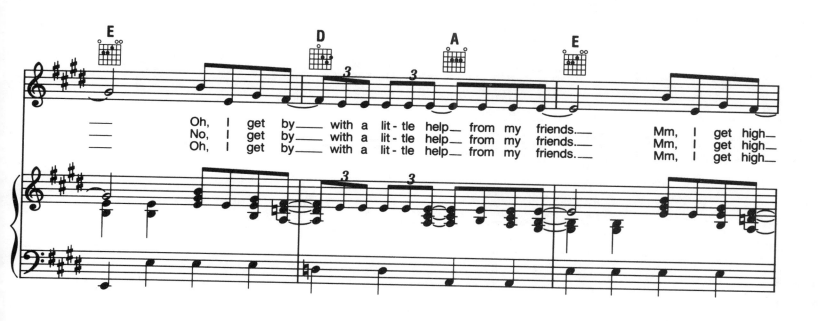

Oh, I get by___ with a lit-tle help___ from my friends.___ Mm, I get high___
No, I get by___ with a lit-tle help___ from my friends.___ Mm, I get high___
Oh, I get by___ with a lit-tle help___ from my friends.___ Mm, I get high___

___ with a lit-tle help___ from my friends.___ Mm, I'm gon-na try___
___ with a lit-tle help___ from my friends.___ Mm, I'm gon-na try___
___ with a lit-tle help___ from my friends.___ Oh, I'm gon-na try___

WONDERFUL TONIGHT

Words and Music by
ERIC CLAPTON

It's late in the eve - ning;
We go to a par - ty,
It's time to go home ___ now,

she's won-d'ring what clothes ___ to wear. ___
and ev-'ry-one turns ___ to see ___
and I've got an ach - ing head. ___

She puts on her make -
this beau-ti-ful la -
So I give her the car ___

YOU'RE MY BEST FRIEND

Words and Music by
JOHN DEACON

With a beat

mf

Dm7 (C bass)   C   F (C bass)

1. Ooh, you make me live____
2. Ooh, you make me live____

What - ev - er this world can
When - ev - er this world is

mf

C   Dm7 (C bass)   C

give to me.____ It's you, you're all I____ see.____
cruel to me.____ I got you to help me for - give.____

Dm7 (C bass)   C   Dm7 (C bass)

Ooh, you make me live____ now, hon - ey, Ooh, you make me live.____
Ooh, you make me live____ now, hon - ey, Ooh, you make me live.____

YOU AIN'T SEEN NOTHIN' YET

Words and Music by
RANDY BACHMAN